THE HOW AND WHY WONDER BOOK

The MICROSCOPE

AND WHAT YOU SEE

Written by MARTIN KEEN

Illustrated by WALTER FERGUSON

Editorial Production: DONALD D. WOLF

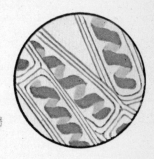

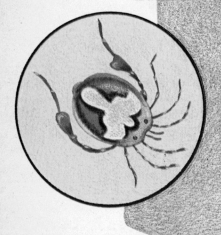

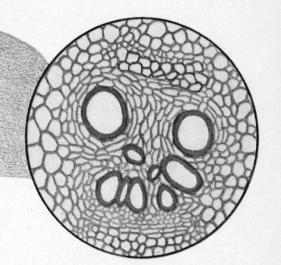

Edited under the supervision of
Dr. Paul E. Blackwood
Washington, D. C.

Text and illustrations approved by
Oakes A. White
Brooklyn Children's Museum
Brooklyn, New York

WONDER BOOKS • NEW YORK
A Division of GROSSET & DUNLAP, Inc.

Introduction

The How and Why Wonder Book of the Microscope introduces one of the instruments that has been most important to scientists in their never-ending search for accurate knowledge about our world. The instrument helps our eyes, wonderful as they are, to be even more wonderful, by extending the sense of sight. It brings before our eyes the world of invisible life, the world of tiniest plants and animals, the *bacteria* and *protozoa*. Indeed, the microscope makes the "unseen world" visible.

But to get full pleasure and benefit from this remarkable instrument requires knowledge of how to operate it carefully. It requires practice in focusing light and in preparing specimens for examination. This book will help the beginning *microscopist* learn these things. And it gives directions for using the microscope to observe the details of many common things all around us. A page of this book suddenly becomes a mass of stringy fibers, while the surface of a tree leaf becomes a miracle of designs when viewed through a microscope.

Every young scientist has ahead of him many exciting experiences exploring the unseen world. *The How and Why Wonder Book of the Microscope,* like the other publications in the series, is a useful teacher and guide in that exploration.

Paul E. Blackwood

Dr. Blackwood is a professional employee in the U. S. Office of Education. This book was edited by him in his private capacity and no official support or endorsement by the Office of Education is intended or should be inferred.

Contents

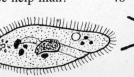

An Unseen World

The human eye is a wonderful organ. Our eyes tell us more about the world around us than any of our other sense organs do. The size and shape of things, their color, their distance from us, and whether one object is in front or in back, above or below, are all things we learn by using our eyes. We can see things that are only a few inches in front of our eyes, and then we can look out the window and instantly see things more than a mile away.

Yet, remarkable as our eyes may be,

there are many things they cannot enable us to see. Among these are very small things. Usually, when we talk about small things, we mean things about the size of the period at the end of this sentence. Now, you can see the period quite easily, and if it were only one-tenth its size, you could still see it. But if the period shrank to one-hundredth of its present size, you would probably lose sight of it. Yet, small as the shrunken period might be, it would still be much larger than millions of

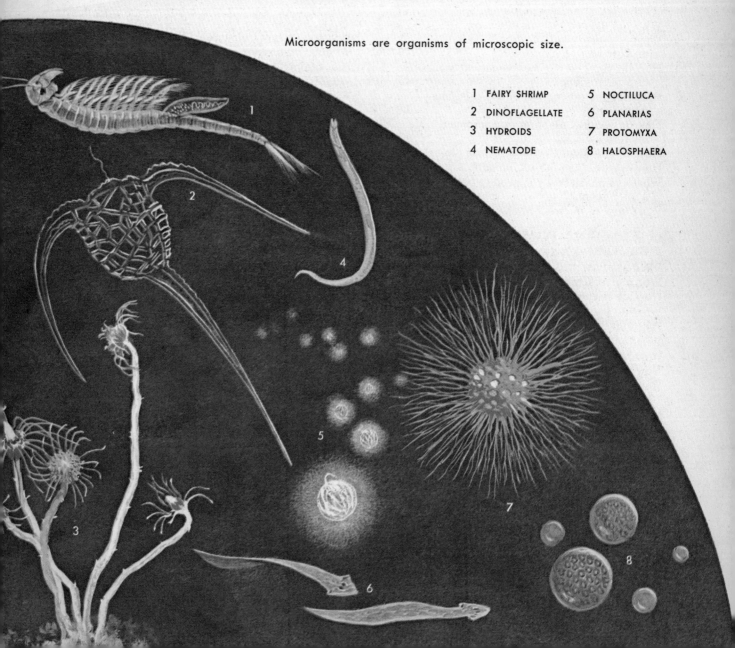

Microorganisms are organisms of microscopic size.

1 FAIRY SHRIMP	5 NOCTILUCA
2 DINOFLAGELLATE	6 PLANARIAS
3 HYDROIDS	7 PROTOMYXA
4 NEMATODE	8 HALOSPHAERA

different kinds of things that exist in your everyday world.

There are certain plants — which we shall soon learn about — that are so small you could put 250,000 of them on the period at the end of this sentence. And there are animals that are not much bigger.

No matter how closely you look at the sheet of paper on which these words are printed, it will still look like a fairly smooth surface, but if your eyes could see much smaller things than they naturally can, you would see that the paper is really a twisted mass of fibers.

There are hundreds of details about the world that are too small for your unaided eyes to see. How, then, do we

learn about these details? What can we use to aid our eyes in seeing the unseen world of very small things that are all around us? We can use an instrument called a *microscope*.

The Microscope

A microscope is an instrument for looking at small things.

What is a microscope?

The word *microscope* comes from two ancient Greek words, *mikros*, which means "small," and *skopein*, which means "to look at."

All microscopes have one thing in common: They contain one or more parts called *lenses*. A lens is any clear substance that has a definite shape and will bend light rays as they pass through it. Most lenses are made of glass, but a lens could be made of water, of oil, or of clear plastic.

When we see anything, we do so because light is reflected from the object to our eyes. If the rays of light come straight from the object to our eyes, we see the object in its natural size. But if the rays of light coming to our eyes are bent in a certain way, then the object looks bigger. When this happens, we say the object is *magnified*. A lens of the proper shape can bend light, so that things we see through the lens are magnified. Any lens that does this is a microscope.

How does it work?

You may wonder if lenses can also

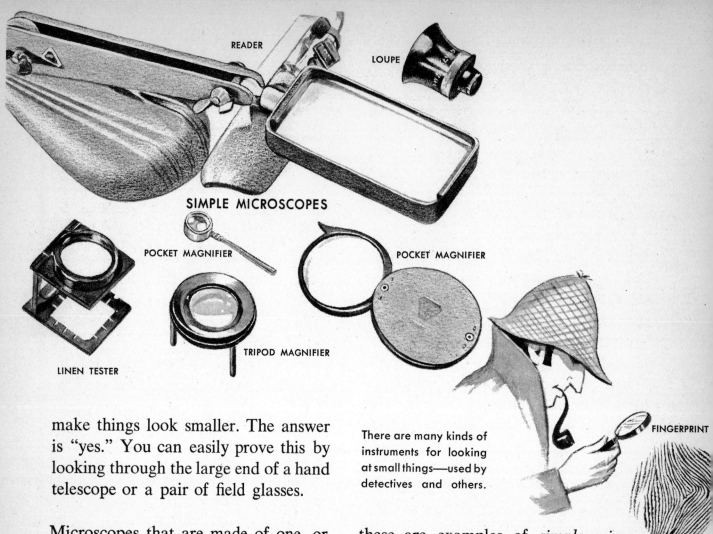

SIMPLE MICROSCOPES

READER

LOUPE

POCKET MAGNIFIER

POCKET MAGNIFIER

LINEN TESTER

TRIPOD MAGNIFIER

FINGERPRINT

There are many kinds of instruments for looking at small things—used by detectives and others.

make things look smaller. The answer is "yes." You can easily prove this by looking through the large end of a hand telescope or a pair of field glasses.

Microscopes that are made of one, or perhaps two, lenses are usually called *magnifying glasses,* or *hand lenses*. These are proper names for them, but they are also microscopes. Have you ever seen the magnifying glass used by stamp collectors? It is made up of just one or two small lenses fixed in a metal frame and held in the hand of the person using it. Have you ever seen a jeweler or a watchmaker looking at a gem or a watch through a black, snouty-looking object held at one eye? This is a microscope called a *loupe*. Did you ever see a picture of the detective Sherlock Holmes holding a round magnifying glass fixed in a circular band of metal and attached to a short handle? All

What is a simple microscope?

these are examples of *simple microscopes*. A simple microscope is one that is made up of one or more lenses that show you a magnified object right-side-up and in the same place where you would see it without the lens. You will understand this definition better when we learn about the other kind of microscope.

You can buy a single- or double-lens microscope in almost any toy store or five-and-ten-cent store. Such microscopes range in price from less than a dollar to three or four dollars. The very cheap ones may have poorly-made glass lenses or plastic lenses that scratch easily. A dollar and a half is probably the price for which you can buy a very useful hand lens, such as is used by stamp collectors.

When you have obtained your simple microscope, you can

What can you see with a simple microscope?

use it to learn things about your daily world that you never knew before. Obtain a magazine with a smooth, or slick, paper cover that bears the color photograph of a person. The majority of the slick paper magazines have covers like this. With your microscope, examine the face of the person in the picture. You will see that the color of the flesh of the face is made up of many tiny dots or specks of different colors. There are red, yellow, and green or blue dots, and the white color of the page shows through in spaces no bigger than the colored dots. Take the magnifying lens away and look at the page with your unaided eye. You will see how the combination of these dots, too small to be seen without the microscope, blends together to produce the color of flesh.

With the microscope, look at the red area of the cheek or at the lips. You will see that there are more red dots crowded closer together in order to produce the redder color.

Open your handkerchief and look at it as you hold it up to the light. You can easily see that it is woven of thou-

A swatch of wool under a microscope shows its weave.

Cotton gabardine twill as viewed under a microscope.

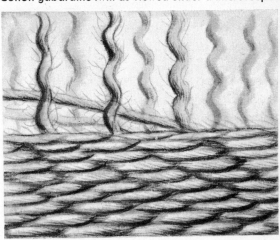

Newspaper print looks like this when it is magnified.

sands of threads. Now use your microscope to look at the handkerchief. You will see how each thread is woven, first under, then over, the threads near it. Note that all the threads are not equally thick. You will see that most of the threads look fuzzy because from their sides tiny, frayed filaments of fiber stick out.

Look at several different samples of

7

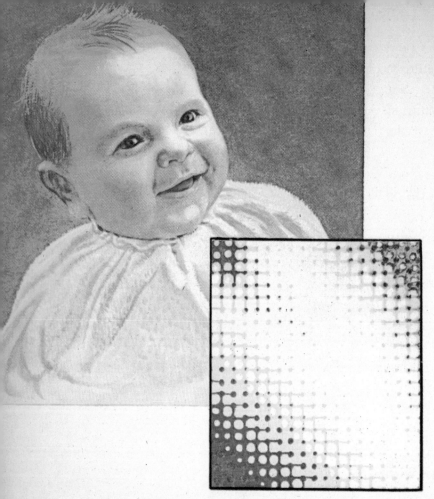

Amethyst crystal when magnified.

When you look at this print of a baby under a microscope, you can see that it is made up of many dots.

cloth that have colored patterns. How can you tell which samples have the color printed on them and which have the color woven into them? You can do this by tracing a single thread with your microscope. If, as far as you can follow the thread, it is one color, then the cloth has a woven pattern. On the other hand, if you trace a single thread and find that it is colored differently in different parts of the pattern, then the pattern was printed on the cloth.

Your microscope will reveal hundreds of new things, if you carefully examine the objects of your daily world. Examine a stone that has different colors in it. Look at the small hairs on the back of your hand. Examine a piece of wood along the surface where a carpenter has sawed it. Look at the leg of an insect.

You will add greatly to your interest and knowledge when working with a microscope, if you keep a record of what you see. You can keep such a record in a notebook or on file cards that are five inches long and three inches wide. Both the notebook and the cards can be bought in almost any stationery or five-and-ten-cent store.

How can you keep a record of what you see?

Here are the things to put in your record book or cards:

Examination number . . .
Date of examination . . .
Object examined . . .
Where I found it . . .
What I saw . . .
Remarks . . .

Under remarks, you might want to

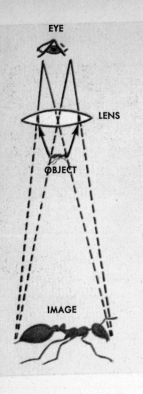

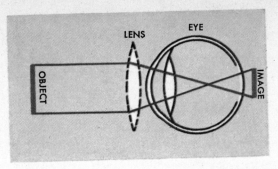

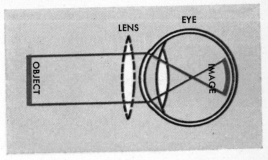

An image out of focus (left).

Image now in focus (right).

Diagram (left): light passing through simple microscope.

write something like: "Compare this with Examination number ___." For example, you may have just examined the antenna of a butterfly, and some time before, you had examined the antenna of a moth. You would probably want to make note of the fact that the antennas of these two kinds of insects are quite different. So, on the card bearing your record of the examination of the butterfly's antenna, you refer to the card bearing the record of the examination of the moth's antenna; and on the moth's card, you refer to the butterfly. Cross-references like this will greatly increase your knowledge of the things you examine.

When you were examining things with your simple microscope, **What is a focus?** you probably noticed that you could not see clearly when you held the lens just any old distance from the object. You had to move the lens back and forth until the object became clear. Why was this necessary?

Your eye has a lens. This lens covers the part of your eye that is colored and also the dark spot, the pupil, at its center. Like all lenses, the one in your eye bends rays of light. The light is bent so that it falls on the back of your eye where light-sensitive materials are located. When the lens in your eye works just right, it bends light so that each light ray entering your eye from an object falls exactly in the proper place to give a sharp image of the object on the back of the eye. As long as the point where the light rays form a sharp image is exactly on the back of the eye, we see the object sharply and clearly. If this point is too far forward or too far back, objects we see are fuzzy and blurred. This is what happens to near- and far-sighted persons. The point at which a lens forms a sharp image is called the *focus* of the lens.

The lens of your microscope also has a focus. You had to move the microscope back and forth until the focus of its lens was exactly where it could work

9

with the lens in your eye, so as to form a sharp image on the back of your eye. We call the moving back and forth of a lens to form a sharp image *focusing* the lens.

How can you make a water-lens microscope? With a pair of pliers, straighten out a paper clip or a piece of wire of similar thickness. At one end of the wire, bend a complete loop about one-sixteenth of an inch across. Rub a little grease or cooking oil on the loop. Dip the loop in water and gently remove it. Within the loop will be a drop of water that forms a lens. Look at the print on a page through the water lens. The lens will probably magnify the print to twice its natural size. Eventually, the water will evaporate, but it is easy to make another water lens.

A different kind of microscope with a water lens can also be made. With a heavy shears, cut a strip from a tin can. This tin strip should be about one inch wide and four inches long. Be careful not to cut yourself on the sharp edges of the tin. When the strip is cut, dull the edges with a file, or cover the edges with adhesive tape.

Mark the exact center of the tin strip. Place the strip on a piece of wood, and drive a medium-size nail through the center. Do not use a nail that will make a hole more than one-sixteenth inch in diameter. Remove the nail and the piece of wood.

Bend the ends of the strip downward, so that the strip will stand. As with the loop microscope, rub a little grease or oil around the hole in the strip. Stand the strip on its two ends. Dip a pencil in water and carefully remove it. Transfer a drop of water from the end of the pencil to the hole, so that a drop hangs in the hole, forming a lens.

Place a small pane of window glass on the tops of two tin cans of the same

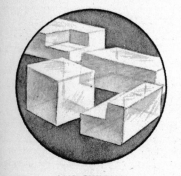

SALT CRYSTALS
MAGNIFIED

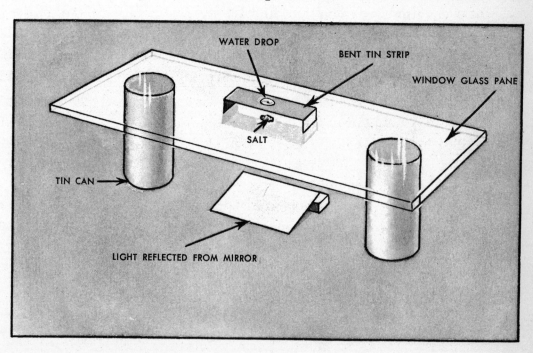

WATER DROP • BENT TIN STRIP • WINDOW GLASS PANE • TIN CAN • SALT • LIGHT REFLECTED FROM MIRROR

The first microscopist was Antony van Leeuwenhoek, a cloth merchant from Holland. He is pictured here with the microscope of his design. (b. 1632; d. 1723)

size. Place the tin strip carefully on the center of the glass. Beneath the glass, prop a flat mirror, such as is found in lady's handbags, so that light is reflected upward through the glass and the water lens.

Beneath the lens, place a few grains of pepper, salt, or sugar, and look down through the lens. Focus the lens by gently pressing on the strip. How many times do you think the water lens magnified the grains?

We don't know just who made the first microscope. In the

Who invented the microscope?

thirteenth century, a monk named Roger Bacon learned how to grind glass to make spectacles. A little while afterward, gentlemen carried about with them a small microscope that consisted of a metal tube, about the size of your thumb, with

a lens at one end. These were called flea glasses or fly glasses, and these names show pretty well what these microscopes were used for.

Although we do not know who invented

What is a microscopist?

the microscope, we do know who was the first *microscopist*. A microscopist is a person who uses a microscope to study small things in a careful and systematic way. If you study things carefully with your simple microscope and keep a record of your findings, you are a microscopist. The first microscopist was Antony van Leeuwenhoek.

Van Leeuwenhoek was a cloth merchant who lived in Delft, Holland during most of the seventeenth century and part of the eighteenth. He lived a quiet life as a tradesman, but he was, in his spare time, one of the world's great scientific discoverers.

11

He obtained diamond dust from the diamond cutters of Delft with which he ground a nearly-spherical lens. He mounted the lens on a device that included a metal rod into which a screw-thread was cut. By turning the rod, he could make very fine focusing adjustments for his lens. The lens and the focusing device were both attached to a metal plate that had a hole in it, just below the lens. By placing objects beneath the hole, van Leeuwenhoek could magnify them as much as 300 times their natural size.

How was diamond dust used for a microscope?

GRASS
SEEDLING

He was fascinated by the world of tiny things that his microscope opened up for him, and spent hours examining all sorts of things around him and writing careful reports on what he saw. He put many of his reports into letters that he sent to the Royal Society of London, an association made up of scientists. The scientists marveled at what van Leeuwenhoek wrote. They honored him by making their own microscopes and imitating his observations.

LOUSE

He hired an illustrator, called a limner, who joined him in his observations and then made drawings of what they both saw. One time van Leeuwenhoek put a louse under his microscope. This little animal was too active to observe well, so van Leeuwenhoek removed its head. However, the louse's legs kept kicking for more than an hour. Meanwhile, as van Leeuwenhoek wrote in his notes, "the Limner could not admire the sight enough, and it took him a long time to put his hand to paper."

GRASS
SPIKELET

He studied the eyes of a shrimp, codfish, whale, rabbit, cow, and beetle. He studied the eggs of ants and lice. Seeds, blossoms, fruits, and other parts of the plant; the circulation of blood in the tail of a fish; the tartar on the teeth of an eight-year-old boy and two ladies; vinegar eels, crabs, and oyster eggs — all these were among the things van Leeuwenhoek placed beneath his microscope.

What objects did he study?

When he was eighty-five, he discovered that "some hundreds of nerves equal the size of a single hair of a man's beard!" And when he was past ninety, he was studying "the wonderful perfections and formations" in the eye of a fly.

With his simple microscope, his careful work, and his enthusiasm, Antony van Leeuwenhoek opened up a world that eventually led to the conquest of many diseases and an understanding of how the many things in the world are constructed.

The Compound Microscope

When most people hear the word "microscope," they usually think of the kind that is seen in laboratories. This microscope, as seen from the outside, has a heavy metal foot, a platform on which to place what is being examined, a nosepiece that points at the platform, and a long tube

What is a compound microscope?

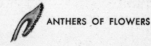

ANTHERS OF FLOWERS

Part of a feather magnified (below); how light rays pass through a compound microscope (right); a compound microscope (far right) with its parts indicated.

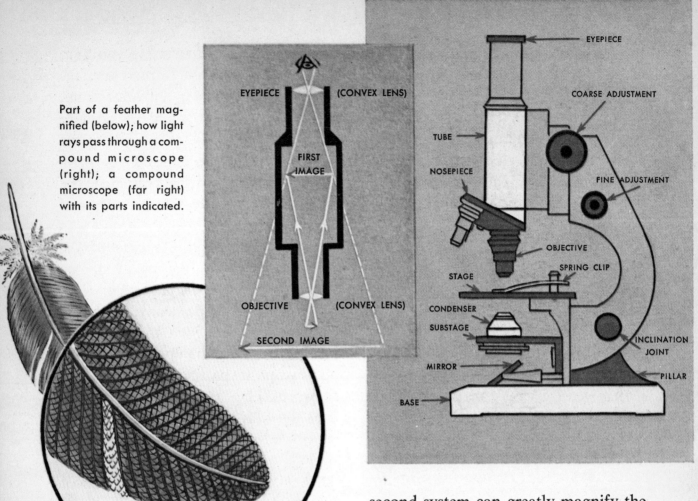

second system can greatly magnify the image and locate it just at the platform of the microscope.

Let us examine the compound laboratory microscope in order to learn its parts. First, let us examine the part through which light passes. Right above the platform, which is properly called the *stage,* is a narrow tube that contains lenses. This tube is called the *objective.* The microscope may have only one objective that fits into a wider tube, called the *nosepiece.* However, most laboratory microscopes have two or three objectives attached to a rotating nosepiece. With this arrangement, the microscopist need only turn

What are some parts of a compound microscope?

at the top of which the microscopist places his eye. This kind of microscope is called a *biological microscope,* or a *laboratory microscope.* It is also a *compound microscope.*

In a compound microscope, there are many lenses. These lenses are grouped into two systems. One system does exactly what a simple microscope does — it shows an upright image, just as the eye would see it, only larger. The focus of this set of lenses is at a point where the

What are the two systems of lenses?

the nosepiece to the right location in order to bring into use the objective he wants.

You may wonder why a microscope would have more than one objective. Each objective has a different magnifying power. The microscopist chooses the objective which magnifies that amount which best enables him to observe what he is looking at. If you look closely at the objectives of a laboratory microscope, you will see marked on one 10x, on the second 43x, and on the third 97x. The "x" means "times" and stands for just what it does in multiplication. An objective with 43x on it means that its lenses will magnify 43 times natural size.

Above the nosepiece, is a wide *tube*. It

How do you find out the magnifying power of a microscope?

is usually empty, but sometimes one or two special lenses are within the tube. Fitting into the upper part of it is a narrower tube called the *extension tube*. This one contains lenses. The lenses in the upper portion together make up the *eyepiece,* or *ocular*. On the ocular, you will see its magnifying power marked. Usually, this is 5x or 10x. If you use a 10x ocular with a 43x objective, the microscope has a total magnifying power of 10 x 43, or 430. In short, to know what the magnifying power of a microscope is, you multiply the power of the ocular by the power of the objective.

What are the other parts of a compound microscope?

The parts of the microscope you have just learned are the most important, but it would be hard to use them without the other parts of a modern microscope. At the bottom of the microscope, is a broad, heavy metal *base,* sometimes called the *foot*. This base holds the working parts of the microscope steady. Rising from the back of the base is the *pillar*. This, too, holds the microscope steady, but at the top of the pillar is a joint, the *inclination joint,* that allows the upper part of the microscope to be tilted backward and forward. The large curved part that does the tilting is called the *arm*. The upper end of the arm holds the tube, while the lower end holds the *stage*. Affixed to the stage are two strips of springy steel. They are called *clips*, and their task is to hold specimens on the stage, especially when the stage is tilted. On more expensive microscopes, the stage is made in two layers. The upper layer can be moved forward or backward, or to the right or left, by turning pairs of knobs.

Where the tube meets the arm is a very important mechanism — the *adjustment*. There is a *coarse adjustment* and a *fine adjustment*. You remember the screw-threaded rod that van Leeuwenhoek fitted to his simple microscope. The coarse and the fine adjustments both consist of very accurately machined screw threads, by means of

GLOEOCAPSA

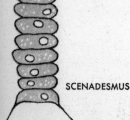
SCENADESMUS

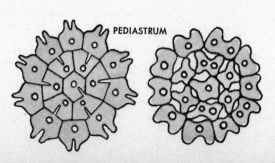
PEDIASTRUM

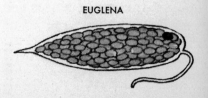
EUGLENA

which the tubes and objectives can be raised and lowered, in order to focus the microscope.

At the very bottom of the arm, a *mirror* is affixed, so that a beam of light can be shined up, through a hole in the stage, to the bottom of the objective, and from there, through the tubes to the eyepiece. Between the mirror and the stage, some microscopes have a third system of lenses to better concentrate the light from the mirror. This system is called a *substage condenser*.

Suppose you wish to examine a hair from your head. First, place on the stage a *glass slide,* which is a piece of clear glass one inch wide and three inches long, and about half as thick as window glass. Push the slide under the clips, so that it is held firmly. Then cut a one-inch length of hair and place it on the slide right above the hole in the stage. Your breath might easily blow the hair away, so fix it in place. This is best done with a material called *Canada balsam.* However, if you have no balsam, use clear household cement or clear fingernail polish.

How do you use a laboratory compound microscope?

Put a small drop of balsam on top of the hair. Wait a few moments in the hope that any tiny bubbles in the balsam will rise to the surface and burst. Don't wait too long, for Canada balsam (and household cement and fingernail polish) harden in air. So gently place on the balsam a very thin piece of glass, about one inch square, called a *cover glass* or *cover slip.* If you see bubbles beneath the cover glass, gently press down upon the cover glass with the tip of a pair of tweezers or a tooth pick. This should help to expel the bubbles. Now the hair is properly *mounted.*

Next, take care of the lighting. To do this, look at the stage from the side, and with the coarse adjustment, move the bottom of the objective to a point about one-sixteenth of an inch above the cover glass. If the microscope has more than one objective, use the one with the lowest magnifying power. When the objective is positioned close to the slide, look into the eyepiece. With one hand, move the mirror about until you see a bright, evenly-lit circle of light, not glaring, not dim. Now you are ready to focus.

Preparing a slide for the microscope properly will make viewing easier.

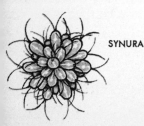

SYNURA

ZYGNEMA

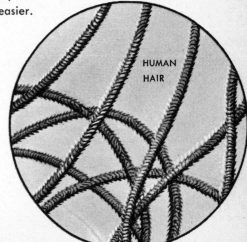

HUMAN HAIR

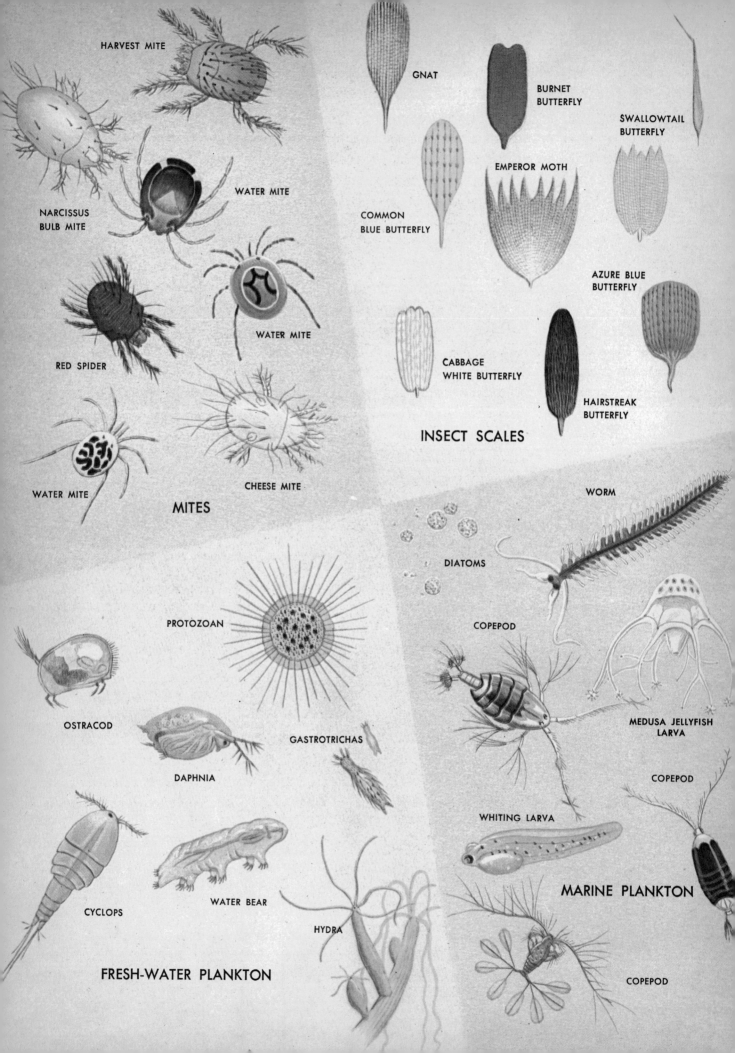

HARVEST MITE

WATER MITE

NARCISSUS
BULB MITE

RED SPIDER

WATER MITE

WATER MITE

CHEESE MITE

MITES

GNAT

BURNET
BUTTERFLY

SWALLOWTAIL
BUTTERFLY

EMPEROR MOTH

COMMON
BLUE BUTTERFLY

AZURE BLUE
BUTTERFLY

CABBAGE
WHITE BUTTERFLY

HAIRSTREAK
BUTTERFLY

INSECT SCALES

WORM

DIATOMS

PROTOZOAN

COPEPOD

OSTRACOD

GASTROTRICHAS

MEDUSA JELLYFISH
LARVA

DAPHNIA

COPEPOD

WHITING LARVA

CYCLOPS

WATER BEAR

MARINE PLANKTON

HYDRA

FRESH-WATER PLANKTON

COPEPOD

When focusing, you must *always* keep
How do you focus it? in mind this rule:
Never focus downward. Always focus upward. If you focus downward, you will surely, sooner or later, push the front of the objective through the slide. This will not only break the slide, and perhaps ruin a valuable specimen, but it may also break the front lens of the objective. Mindful of this, turn slowly the coarse adjustment toward yourself, so that the tube rises from the slide. When the hair comes clearly into view, change from the coarse adjustment to the fine one. Although you must turn the coarse adjustment only in one direction when focusing, you may turn the fine adjustment in either direction, *as long as you do not turn it more than half a turn.* Thus, with the fine adjustment, you can bring the hair into clear focus. You will probably find that you have to adjust the mirror again.

After you have studied the hair for a while, you may want to magnify it more. If the microscope has only one nosepiece, raise the objective far above the slide, unscrew the objective to take it out of the nosepiece, and then put another, higher-power, objective into the nosepiece. Then focus in the same way as you did when using the low-power objective.

Illustrated on the left are other specimens which may be viewed under the microscope. Mites belong to a family of tiny animals related to spiders and scorpions. They often infest other animals, including humans, plants, and foods. Protozoa, along with other tiny animals, as well as plants, make up the plankton, which floats on the surface of oceans and lakes. Plankton serves as the food for many forms of sea life.

If the microscope has a nosepiece with two objectives, simply turn the lower part of the nosepiece around so that the other objective is in line with the tube. If the microscope is well made, changing the objective should not change the focus very much. However, some focusing with the fine adjustment will probably be necessary. Also, you will have to adjust the lighting again.

If the microscope has a third objective, move it into place just as you did the second one. However, you cannot use this objective simply by focusing. This objective, usually the one marked 97x, is an *oil immersion lens*. It has this name because to use it, you usually put the foremost lens of the objective into a drop of oil placed upon the cover glass. Again you will have to focus, and this time be very careful, because the front of the objective is nearly touching the cover glass. The oil you use must be *cedarwood oil*. This oil can be obtained from microscope dealers.

After examining the hair, you will have to clean the equipment.
How do you clean the equipment? Turn the coarse adjustment knob to raise the oil immersion lens from the slide. Then wet a special kind of tissue, called *lens tissue,* in a liquid called *xylol.* With the wetted tissue, wipe all the oil off the oil immersion lens. It is well to use two separate pieces of tissue for two wipings. The xylol evaporates quickly, but may leave a foggy deposit on the lens, so wipe the lens with a dry piece of lens tissue.

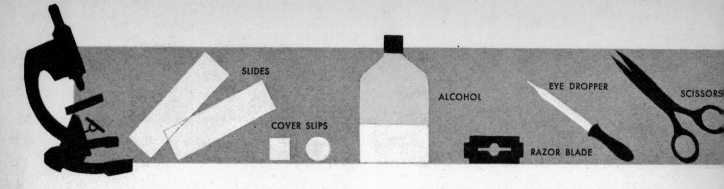

SLIDES

COVER SLIPS

ALCOHOL

EYE DROPPER

RAZOR BLADE

SCISSORS

If you wish to keep the slide with the mounted hair, wipe off with xylol any excess balsam that has oozed out from under the cover glass, label the slide, and store it. If, on the other hand, you do not wish to keep the slide mount, place a drop or two of xylol around the edges of the cover glass. This will work its way under the glass and dissolve the balsam so that you can remove the cover glass. Now all you have to do is wipe the cover glass and the slide with some xylol or lens tissue.

If you want to make microscopy your hobby, you will have to start with certain basic equipment: a microscope; glass slides (at least a dozen to begin with); cover glasses (about two dozen, since these break very easily); tweezers (or forceps); a medicine dropper; a probe (made by sticking the eye-end of a needle into an eraser removed from a pencil); a sharp knife, or single-edge razor blade; sharp-pointed scissors; Canada balsam (or fingernail polish); and xylol (or acetone). While a simple microscope will reveal many wonders of the world around you, this instrument has its limits. You cannot buy one that will give the 300x power of van Leeuwenhoek's. Even a good simple

What equipment will you need to become a microscopist?

microscope will not magnify more than 10x, and the very best will magnify only 20x. In order to really do interesting work in microscopy, you need a compound microscope.

A laboratory, or biological, compound microscope is a very expensive instrument that costs several hundred dollars. However, it is possible to purchase a so-called *amateur microscope* which is much less expensive. This is a smaller model of the laboratory microscope. It lacks some refinements that only a highly-trained scientist would need for his work, but in your microscopy, you will not miss them at all. These amateur microscopes are not toys — they are real compound microscopes that will produce a clear image magnified 300 to 500 times. You can buy such a microscope for $11 to $20. This may seem like quite a lot of money, but if you begin immediately to put away nickels and dimes that you find you really do not have to spend, you will have saved up the needed money sooner than now seems likely. When you are ready to buy your microscope, you will be wise to consult a science teacher in your school. He can give you advice on how to go about buying the microscope. One good place to buy an amateur mi-

What kind of microscope should you get?

18

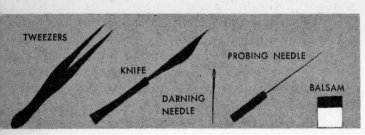

TWEEZERS
KNIFE
DARNING NEEDLE
PROBING NEEDLE
BALSAM

SNOW CRYSTALS MAGNIFIED

croscope is from a mail-order house. Consult its catalog carefully before you order. Make sure there is a guarantee that the microscope will be replaced if it is defective when you get it.

The World of Invisible Life — Bacteria and Protozoa

What are the smallest plants in the world?

All around us are billions of tiny living things that are too small to be seen with the unaided eyes. Among the smallest of these living things are plants called *bacteria*. A single one of these plants is a *bacterium*. Some bacteria are so small that 10,000 of them could be placed on the period at the end of this sentence.

Each bacterium is a single living cell. This means that it is a separate bit of living matter that can live and grow by itself. It can take into itself food and oxygen. It uses the food for nourishment, and the oxygen to help it nourish itself, grow and move.

Where are bacteria found?

Bacteria may be found all around us — in the earth, in water and in the air. There are millions of bacteria on your skin, in your mouth, your nasal passages, and elsewhere inside your body. There are thousands of different kinds of bacteria. They are man's invisible friends and foes. They are both useful and harmful to man.

How are bacteria useful?

Among the useful bacteria are those that produce buttermilk and vinegar, age cheese, and help in the curing of leather. Probably the most valuable service that bacteria give to

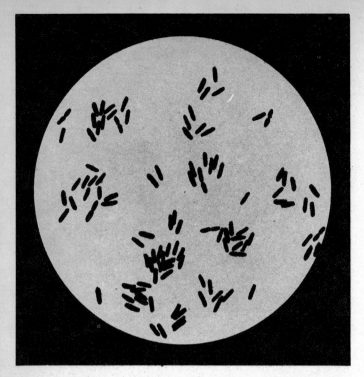

Bacilli, rod-shaped bacteria, may be useful or harmful.

and forth rapidly and push the bacterium through the liquid. Some bacteria have cilia growing out from all parts of the cell wall. Others have just a single thread at one or both ends. Still others have a tuft of cilia at one end.

Since bacteria are so important to man, it is useful to know in what conditions bacteria live and grow. Most bacteria thrive best at the temperature of the human body — a little

When do they thrive best?

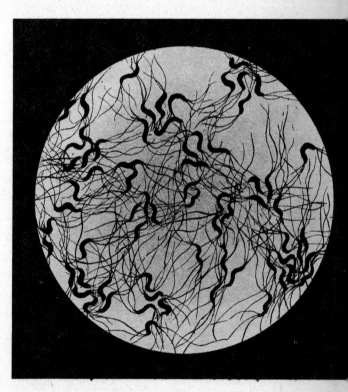

Some spirilla, spiral bacteria, have thread-like ends.

man is to cause decay. If decay bacteria were not constantly at work, the earth would become littered with the dead bodies of animals and plants.

Harmful bacteria are those that cause disease in animals and plants. Among the diseases caused in man by bacteria are pneumonia, typhoid fever and tuberculosis. Fortunately, there are more harmless bacteria than harmful ones.

Bacteria may have any one of three shapes. Some are round like a ball. A bacterium of this shape is called a *coccus*. Another kind of bacterium is shaped like a rod, and is called a *bacillus*. The third kind of bacterium has a spiral shape, and is called a *spirillum*.

What do bacteria look like?

Some bacteria can move when they are in a liquid. A bacterium of this kind has extremely thin threads of living matter growing out from its cell wall. These threads, called *cilia*, lash back

less than 99 degrees Fahrenheit. Both lower and higher temperatures slow the growth of bacteria. Freezing and boiling will kill most bacteria. You can now see that putting food in the refrigerator slows the growth of bacteria that may be on the food, and thereby prevents the food from becoming spoiled. Also,

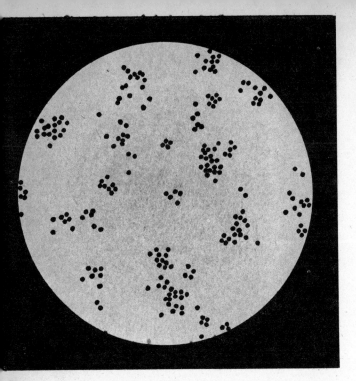

Cocci are ball-like, or spherically-shaped, bacteria.

Bacteria reproduce themselves very rapidly. It takes only about thirty minutes for one bacterium to become two. If all the offspring of one bacterium could go on reproducing for twelve hours, there would be seventeen million of them. If this process continued for five days, bacteria would fill all the oceans to a depth of one mile. Of course, nothing like this can take place, because most bacteria do not find the nourishment or favor-

How fast do bacteria reproduce?

cooking food not only makes it easier and tastier to eat, but also kills harmful bacteria that may be on it.

Bacteria need much moisture in order to thrive. Thus, if we keep food dry, we keep it from spoiling by the growth of bacteria upon it. Darkness is another condition in which bacteria thrive. A strong light will slow the growth of bacteria or kill them. Now you can see why a sunny room is a healthy room.

In most civilized countries, the law requires that bacteria in milk be killed by raising the temperature of the milk to 145 degrees Fahrenheit and keeping it at this temperature for thirty minutes. This process for killing bacteria is called *pasteurization* and was discovered by the great French bacteriologist Louis Pasteur. A bacteriologist is a scientist who studies and works with bacteria — or the science of bacteriology.

What is the process of pasteurization?

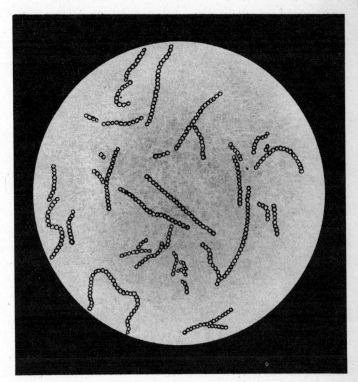

Cocci may also grow in pairs, clusters or in chains.

able conditions in which to grow and reproduce.

One of the best ways to get harmless bacteria is to make a *hay infusion*. Fill a two-quart glass jar almost full of water. If you can get water

How can you get bacteria?

9:00 A.M.   9:20 A.M.   9:40 A.M.   10:00 A.M.

Many bacteria reproduce by splitting in two — a half hour process. Some split in 20 min.

from a stream or lake, you can proceed immediately with the rest of the experiment. If you take water from a tap, allow the jar to stand uncovered for three days, so that excess oxygen that is probably dissolved in the water may escape. Paste a label on the outside of the jar at the level of the surface of the water, so that you may add more water to the jar, if needed. Add only water that you have allowed to stand for a while, like the original jar.

Cut a handful of hay or dry grass into short lengths and put it into the water in the jar. Cover the jar and place it where daylight, but not direct sunlight, will reach it. In about three or four days, you will notice a scum on the surface of the water and an accompanying unpleasant odor. The scum is formed by billions of bacteria.

Plunge the tip of your medicine dropper beneath the scum, and **How do you prepare bacteria for the microscope?** draw up some clear water. Place a drop of this water on a glass slide. Using your probe, pick up a very small amount of scum — just enough to cover the point of the needle — and dip the needle into the drop of water on the slide. Place a cover glass over the drop. Focus

carefully and adjust the mirror in several different positions as you seek for bacteria in the field of your microscope. If you see nothing but a blurry blob of material, it means that you have placed too large an amount of scum on the slide. Make a new slide, using only one-tenth as much scum. In trying to find bacteria, the lighting is very important. Spend considerable time in manipulating the mirror. In your report, describe the shapes of the bacteria you see.

There are many other sources of bacteria among everyday things. Imitate Leeuwenhoek by scraping with a tooth-

An organism continues to reproduce in a new culture.

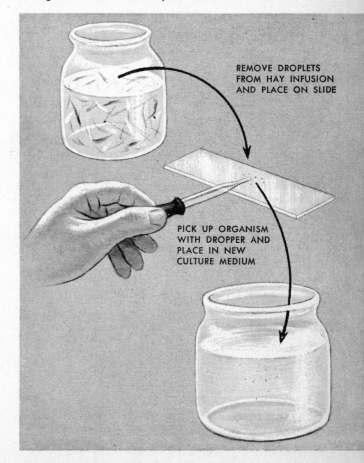

REMOVE DROPLETS FROM HAY INFUSION AND PLACE ON SLIDE

PICK UP ORGANISM WITH DROPPER AND PLACE IN NEW CULTURE MEDIUM

1

2

3

4

5

6

(1) *Streptococci.* (2) *Staphylocci.* (3) *Tetanus bacilli.* (4) *Typhoid bacilli.* (5) *Tuberculosis bacilli.* (6) *Cholera vibrio.* All are disease-causing bacteria in man.

22

pick a tiny bit of the white material from your teeth, just at the gum-line. Place this white material in a drop of water, on a slide. Make a few cuts in a peach or an apple, and let the fruit stand in a warm, damp place for a few days. Place a bit of the material from the cut in a drop of water on a slide, and examine it for bacteria. Mix a pinch of soil in a little water. Place a drop of this mixture on a slide and examine it for bacteria.

Placing bacteria in a drop of water on a slide makes a preparation that requires much manipulation of the mirror in order to be able to see the bacteria at all. This method has the advantage of presenting for examination live bacteria, some of which may be moving. There is, however, another method of preparing bacteria that makes them much easier to see.

How can you stain bacteria? You can prepare a slide of bacteria so that they will be easily seen, if you *stain* the bacteria either red or blue. First, of course, you will need the stain. The blue stain is called *methylene blue,* and the red stain is *eosin.* You can buy both of them from a pharmacist. They are cheap, and you need very little of each. If you buy the stains in dry form, dissolve in half a tumblerful of water just as much of either as you can pick up on the end of a knife blade. This will give you enough to last for months. It is wise to keep the stains in stoppered bottles, so that the water does not evaporate.

Many microorganisms flourish in a hay infusion. Shown are the *colpoda, hay bacillus,* and *volvox,* all magnified.

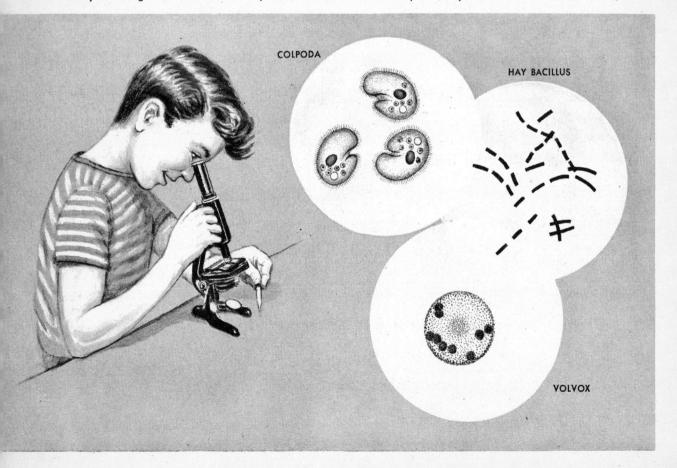

COLPODA

HAY BACILLUS

VOLVOX

If you cannot buy these two stains, you can use ink. For the blue stain use the "permanent" kind of blue fountain pen ink, which contains methylene blue. For red stain use any kind of red ink.

Prepare the stained slide in this manner:

How can you prepare a stained slide? Place a drop of water on a clean slide. Using your probe, add a small amount of the bacteria-containing material to the wa-ter, and spread the mixture into a broad smear. Grasp the slide by the edges near one end, and hold it several inches above a candle flame until the water evaporates. Hold the slide sufficiently high above the flame so that the water does not boil. You do not want to cook the bacteria.

When all of the water has evaporated and the slide is thoroughly dry, pass the slide through the candle flame rapidly three or four times. This action is called *fixing* the smear.

When the slide has cooled thoroughly, drop a stain from your medicine dropper on the fixed smear. Some bacteria stain better with blue dye and others stain better with red dye. You will have to experiment with both colors to see which one best stains the kind of bacteria you are working with.

Leave the stain on the smear for about a minute. Some bacteria will need more than a minute to stain thoroughly. Again, you will have to learn this by experience. After the stain has been on the smear for the proper length of time, wash it off with running tap water. Then, place the slide, smear-side up, on a paper towel. Fold the towel over and blot the slide carefully. Do not rub the towel on the smear. This will destroy the smear. Now, examine the slide under the microscope.

Picture-instructions for preparing a stained slide:

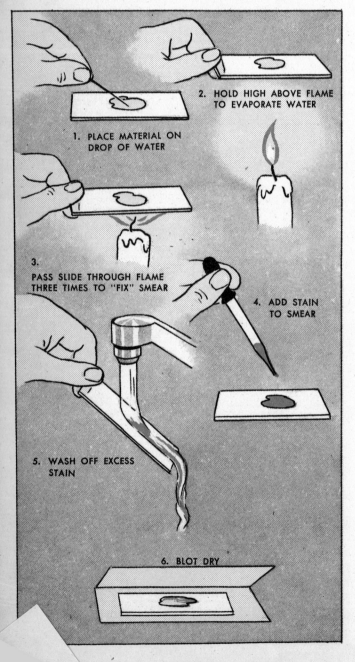

1. PLACE MATERIAL ON DROP OF WATER

2. HOLD HIGH ABOVE FLAME TO EVAPORATE WATER

3. PASS SLIDE THROUGH FLAME THREE TIMES TO "FIX" SMEAR

4. ADD STAIN TO SMEAR

5. WASH OFF EXCESS STAIN

6. BLOT DRY

There is another way to prepare a slide of bacteria, so that you can observe them alive. This is called the *hanging drop* method.

What is a hanging drop mount?

There is a kind of thick glass slide that

has a little well ground into its center. This slide is used to set up a hanging drop mount. Such slides are expensive, so you would probably do best if you make your own hanging drop apparatus.

Cut a piece of cardboard exactly the size of a glass slide. You can do this best by tracing the outline of the slide on the cardboard. Now, cut the cardboard into three equal lengths. With your pointed scissors, cut a hole, no bigger than half an inch, in the center of each of the three pieces of cardboard. Glue the three pieces together, one on top of the other, so that there is a single hole through all three. Cement this cardboard "washer" to the center of a glass slide. Cover one of your fingers lightly with petroleum jelly — like Vaseline. Holding a cover glass in your hand, scrape the jelly off your finger, using all the edges of the cover glass, until there is a rim of jelly all around the edges of the cover glass. Place the glass on the table, jelly-side up. Using your probe, place a mixture of water and a drop of the bacteria-containing material you want to examine on the center of the cover glass.

Hold the glass slide so that the cardboard washer is underneath and the hole in the washer is right over the center of the cover glass. Lower the slide, and press the washer firmly on the jelly rim of the cover glass. Then, with a quick motion, turn the slide over. A drop of the mixture you are to examine

How can you make your own hanging drop mount?

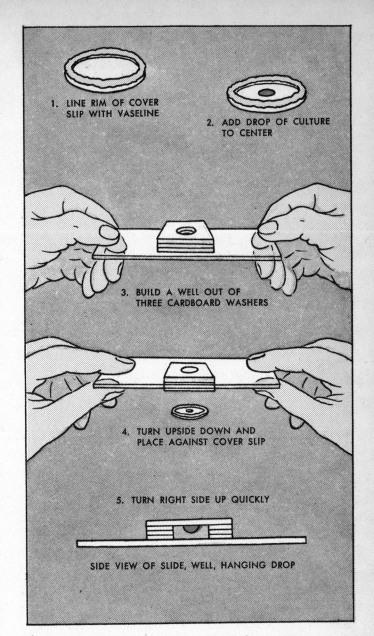

1. LINE RIM OF COVER SLIP WITH VASELINE

2. ADD DROP OF CULTURE TO CENTER

3. BUILD A WELL OUT OF THREE CARDBOARD WASHERS

4. TURN UPSIDE DOWN AND PLACE AGAINST COVER SLIP

5. TURN RIGHT SIDE UP QUICKLY

SIDE VIEW OF SLIDE, WELL, HANGING DROP

Picture-directions for preparing hanging drop mount.

will be hanging down from the cover glass. Examine the drop under the microscope, focusing it carefully.

Perhaps, when you were looking at bacteria from your hay infusion, you saw a large object swim across your field of view. This large object was a one-celled animal of the kind called *protozoa*. This name means "earliest

What are the smallest animals in the world?

easier to find protozoa and a little harder to find bacteria. Also, the amount of scum seemed to lessen. This was because the protozoa were feeding on the bacteria. They increased in number as they ate up the bacteria.

Protozoa are interesting to watch under a microscope because they have so many different forms and they move about in many different ways. You can see them hunting and catching their food, which is usually bacteria, but may

Stagnant water may teem with harmful bacteria and protozoa.

ENTAMOEBA HISTOLYTICA

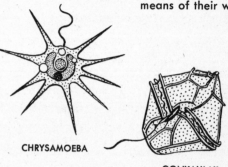

Flagellated protozoa swim by means of their whips.

CHRYSAMOEBA

GONYAULAX

EUGLENA

form of animals" and refers to the fact that protozoa were probably the first animals to appear in the oceans of the earth hundreds of millions of years ago. They are still water animals, and are found in the seas, lakes and streams. A single one of these animals is called a *protozoan*.

A protozoan, like a bacterium, is a separate bit of living matter that can take in and use food, get rid of wastes, move, grow and reproduce. There are thousands of kinds. Most are harmless, but a few are harmful to man. Among the harmful ones are those that cause such diseases as malaria, dysentery and sleeping sickness.

If you worked with your hay infusion

What do the protozoa eat?

for several days, you may have noticed that it became continually

be just bits of once-living plant or animal material floating about in the water — or it may be other protozoa.

The hanging drop method is one of the best ways of preparing a slide for the examination of protozoa. The main difficulty with this method is that the drop provides the tiny animals with such a large ocean to swim in that they swim either above or below the level on which your microscope is focused. One big advantage of the hanging drop mount for protozoa is that the water does not evaporate easily, and you can watch the tiny animals for a long time.

How can you examine protozoa?

Another way to prepare a slide for the observation of protozoa is simply to place a drop of water from a hay infusion on a glass slide and cover it gently with a cover glass. When obtaining the drop, poke your medicine dropper beneath the scum on the surface of the infusion.

The cover glass flattens the drop of water so much that there is very little room for the protozoa to swim up and down. Once you have focused on one of them, it will usually remain in focus for a long time. The main disadvantage of this method of mounting is that the water evaporates quite rapidly. While you are looking at a particularly interesting protozoan, the slide may dry up right under your eyes. You can prevent this from happening by putting a rim of petroleum jelly around the edges of

Ciliated protozoa swim by means of hair-like organs.

STENTOR

DIDIDIUM

STYLONICHIA

the cover glass, *after* it is placed upon the drop of water.

You will find that many protozoa are

How can you keep protozoa in place? simply too active to enable you to get a good look at them, especially when you are using the high-power objective.

One way to keep the protozoa in place is to trap them in the fibers of a piece of thread. Fray a half-inch piece of thread so that the fibers make a mat. Flatten this mat, and place it in the drop of water on the slide, before you put on the cover glass. The fibers will form a "net" that will entangle and hold, or slow down, the protozoa in the water.

You may see one or more protozoa

How do protozoa move about? move around under your microscope, and, unless you know just what to look for, you may be unable to tell just how they move. Some protozoa move through the water by means of cilia along the sides of their bodies. Some protozoans have at one end a thread of living matter that is longer and thicker than a cilium. This thread is called a *flagellum*, a Latin

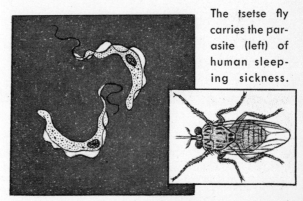

The tsetse fly carries the parasite (left) of human sleeping sickness.

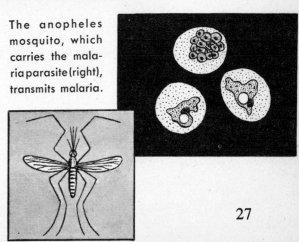

The anopheles mosquito, which carries the malaria parasite (right), transmits malaria.

27

word that means "whip." Some protozoa pull themselves through the water by beating these whips down to their sides. Others use the whip as a tail and push themselves through the water in the same way you can push a small boat along by moving a single oar back and forth in the water behind the boat's stern.

The only whip-bearing protozoan that

What is a Peranema? you are likely to find in a hay infusion is one called *Peranema*. You will recognize this one because it has two whips, a long one and a short one, at opposite ends of the body. You may be puzzled to understand what makes *Peranema* move, when its whips seem to be standing still. If you look closely at the tip of the long one, you will see that it is vibrating back and forth very rapidly. Also, *Peranema* is always changing shape. Sometimes it looks like a radish, sometimes like a bulging potato. To see *Peranema* well, you must use a high-power objective and a rather dim light.

If you scrape the inside of your mouth with a toothpick and make a slide of the material obtained, you may be able to see other whip-bearers. Several kinds live in the human body, and almost all of them are entirely harmless.

Your hay infusion may yield a more or

What is an amoeba? less shapeless protozoan called an *amoeba*. This protozoan has no particular shape. Sometimes it may be nearly round, and at other times it may have a half dozen ragged projections sticking out from the central mass of its body.

You must watch an amoeba for some

How does an amoeba move? time in order to see how it moves. In the first place, it spends a great part of its time resting, or, at least, not moving. Secondly, an amoeba moves very slowly. As you watch, you will see that a projection of living material slowly moves outward from the main part of its body. This projection is called a *pseudopod,* or false foot. Then, you will see more living material streaming into the false foot, which will grow larger. Eventually, all of the amoeba will have streamed into what was a pseudopod, and the whole amoeba will now be at the place to which the pseudopod first reached out.

One of the most common kind of pro-

What is a paramecium? tozoa is a *paramecium*. It is shaped something like a long slipper. Its body is covered with cilia that beat back and forth very rapidly. Since there are hundreds of cilia on the body, and all are acting like tiny oars, the paramecium is moved through the water very rapidly. A paramecium is also one of the largest of the protozoa. It may reach a diameter of more than $1/100$ of an inch. If you see one under your microscope, it might be interesting to remove the slide from the clips and see whether you can see the paramecium with your naked eye. To do this place the slide on a black background, and shine a light directly down upon the cover glass. The paramecia will be seen as bright moving specks.

Protozoa, such as the amoeba and paramecia, are large

What is inside a protozoan? enough so that we not only can study their general form, but we can examine what is inside them.

Since each protozoan is a single living cell, it possesses some of the characteristics of all living cells. It is surrounded by a membrane that holds it together. The living material that is within the cell membrane is called *cytoplasm*. If you examine the cytoplasm carefully, you will see that it looks grainy, as if it were made up of grains of colorless sand. It is this graininess that enables the cytoplasm in the amoeba to stream into its false feet, just as sand in a sack can be made to flow around by moving the sack.

Within the cytoplasm is a large dark dot. This is the cell's *nucleus*. All the movements and activities of the protozoan are directed by it. It is somewhat as though the nucleus were the cell's brain.

Somewhere in the cytoplasm of an amoeba or a para-

How do protozoa collect wastes and water? mecium, you will see one or two (or more) large clear circles. In the paramecium, you may

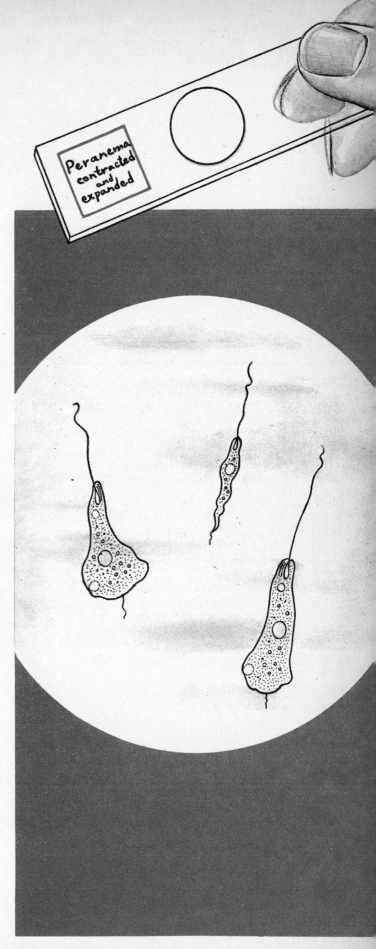

Peranema changes shape by contracting, expanding.

see a clear, star-shaped spot. These are *contractile vacuoles*. They move about within the cytoplasm collecting waste materials and excess water. When they reach the membrane of the protozoan, they suddenly contract and expel their burden outside the cell wall. After this happens, the vacuole becomes very small, but as it moves about picking up waste materials and water, it grows larger.

Also within the cytoplasm, you will **How does the amoeba eat?** probably see small dark dots with lighter circles around them. These are bits of food that the proto-

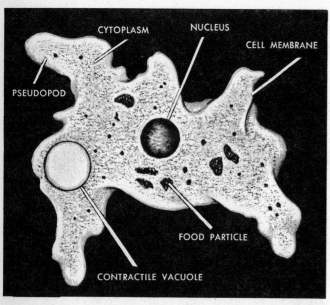

The amoeba is a microscopic, single-celled animal. Its name comes from the Greek word for *change*.

zoan has taken into itself, and it is interesting to watch how this is done. When an amoeba comes upon a bit of food, it reaches out two pseudopods to surround the food particle. When the pseudopods have curved completely around the piece of food, they meet. Then the

membrane between them dissolves, and the food particle is inside the amoeba.

A paramecium has a tougher cell membrane, and cannot, **How does a paramecium get its food?** therefore, put out pseudopods to surround a bit of food. Instead, the paramecium has a mouth and a gullet into which nourishment is taken. If you look closely at a paramecium, you will see a groove along one side, near the front end. This is the *oral groove*. Focus very carefully, and you may be able to see that the oral groove is lined with cilia. When a paramecium comes upon food particles, usually bacteria, the beating of the cilia shove the particles along the oral groove to a point near the middle of the body where there is a tube. The opening of this tube is the *mouth,* and the tube, itself, is the *gullet.* When food particles reach the lower end of the gullet, they collect into a ball, and this ball, along with a little water, floats into the cytoplasm. You see the food as a dark dot, and the water as the light circle around the dot. Together, they make up a *food vacuole.*

Since the feeding actions of protozoa are so interesting, **How can you feed protozoa?** you may want to provide food in order to watch them take it into their bodies. Pick off from a cake of yeast a piece about the size of the eye of a needle. Mash the speck of yeast in a drop of water. Place a little of this mixture in the center of a drop of water that contains protozoa. Place a cover slip on the

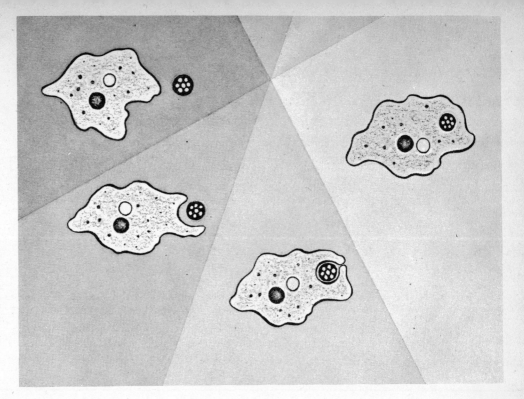

The illustrations show how the pseudopods of an amoeba engulf a particle of food, until the food is completely inside the protozoan.

water. Dip the end of a toothpick into red ink and transfer a small drop of ink to the edge of the cover glass. The red dye in the ink will make it easier for you to see the food-taking activities.

When bacteria or protozoa find themselves in conditions **How do bacteria and protozoa suspend life?** that are too dry, they temporarily suspend their living processes, without actually dying. To accomplish this, they surround themselves with a very tough covering that protects them from completely drying out, and also from sudden changes in temperature. A bacteria in this condition is called a *spore,* and a protozoan is a *cyst.* Spores and cysts are very light and can be easily carried by even the lightest breezes.

When a spore or cyst again happens upon wet conditions, the thick covering dissolves and the bacterium or the protozoan goes on living just as it did before it encountered unfavorable conditions.

Since the grass you used for making a hay infusion was **Where do hay-infusion bacteria and protozoa come from?** dry, you may wonder where water-living creatures like bacteria and protozoa came from after the grass had soaked for a few days. Bacteria and protozoa that had been living on the hay-infusion grass before it dried formed spores and cysts when drying took place. When you placed the grass in water, the walls of the spores and cysts dissolved.

A few days after you put the dry grass into the water, **How do the number of bacteria and protozoa increase?** a scum made up of bacteria appeared in your hay infusion. For a few days, the amount of scum increased, thereby

31

showing that the number of bacteria was increasing. If you examined the water every day, you found that at first there were few protozoa, and then their number increased. Since the number of bacteria and protozoa *increased*, they could not all have been on the grass as spores or cysts. Where did the new ones come from? The bacteria and protozoa reproduced themselves — processes which are very interesting to watch.

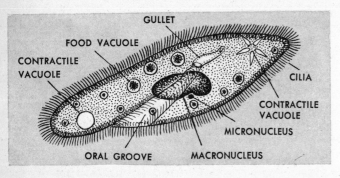

The paramecium swims by means of cilia. It reproduces by splitting or cell division.

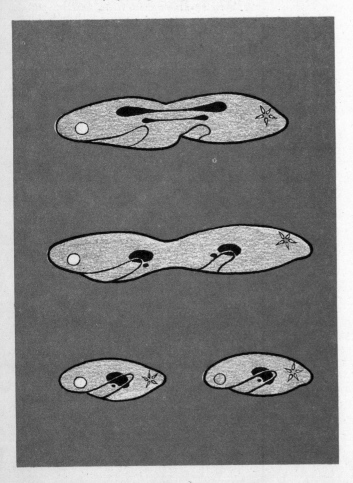

When a bacterium or protozoan begins to reproduce, its nucleus lengthens, narrows in the middle, pinches off to become two nuclei, and then each new nucleus moves to opposite ends of the cell. While the nucleus is going through its splitting process, the whole cell begins to do the same. It lengthens, narrows in the middle, and finally pinches in two. This process lags just a little behind that of the nucleus. The splitting process is called *cell division*. The reproduction of a bacterium takes just about half an hour. This means that you can easily watch the whole process without tiring. The cell division of a protozoan may take longer, but not so long that you cannot watch it.

How do they reproduce?

One of the convenient things about the cell division of a protozoan is that during this process, the little animal hardly moves about. Thus, it is easy to see beneath a microscope. To find a reproducing bacterium or protozoan you must search around carefully on your slide. Move the slide back and forth beneath the microscope's objective. As you have probably already learned, when you move the slide to the right, it seems to move to the left when you look through the microscope. And, of course, when you move the slide to the left, it seems to move to the right. This is confusing, but with a little practice, you can learn to manipulate the slide correctly.

As you watch the process of cell division, continually focus up and down with the fine adjustment on your micro-

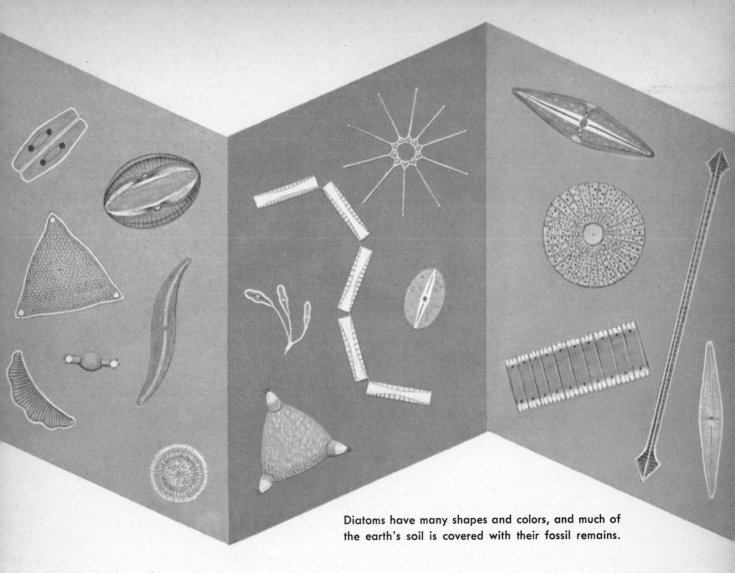

Diatoms have many shapes and colors, and much of the earth's soil is covered with their fossil remains.

scope. By doing this, you may be able to see that other small objects within the cell, besides the nucleus, split and move to opposite ends of the cell. A small drop of red dye or ink will help you to see this part of cell division.

One-celled plants, called *diatoms*, are able to use certain chemicals dissolved in water to build either a shell or a framework of hard glassy material around their soft bodies. Diatoms live in the waters of streams and lakes, oceans and in damp soil. When they die, their tiny glasslike

What kind of microscopic plants live in "houses"?

houses settle to the bottom of the water. Sometimes these little plants live in such great numbers that their tiny shells cover the bottom of bodies of water in thick layers. If the stream or the lake dries up, the layers of diatom shells form a kind of hard earth called *diatomaceous earth.*

If you live near a body of water, you may be able to get specimens of diatoms to examine under your microscope. In streams and lakes, your best chance of finding diatoms is in the mud at the bottom of the water. Take a sample of this mud mixed with water and make microscopic slides from it. Any sample of ocean water may contain diatoms.

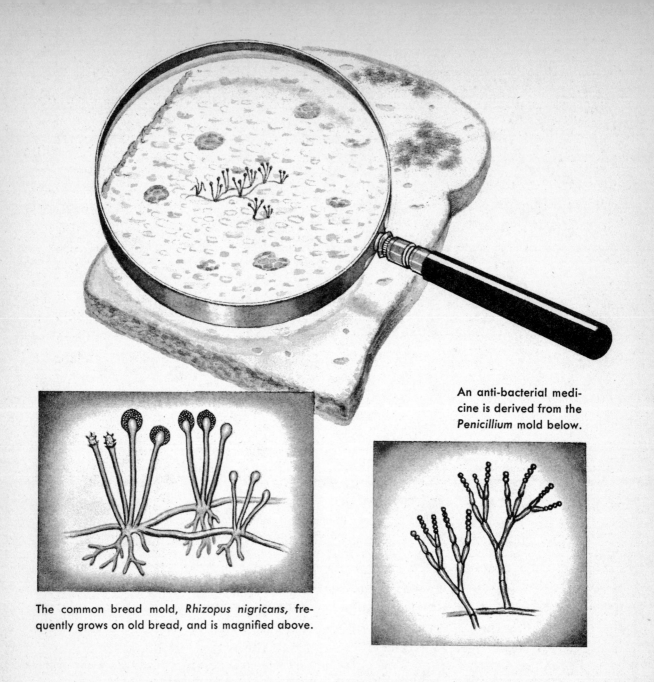

The common bread mold, *Rhizopus nigricans*, frequently grows on old bread, and is magnified above.

An anti-bacterial medicine is derived from the *Penicillium* mold below.

Molds, Mildew, Yeast Budding

How can you grow plants on a slice of bread? Sprinkle water on four or five slices of bread. Wipe the damp side of these slices across the floor, taking care not to crumble the bread. Put the bread into a closet or some other warm, dark place. Two days later, examine the slices. You will probably find on them patches of a white cottony material peppered with black dots. This material is the thick growth of a plant called *common bread mold*.

To examine this mold, place a small piece of bread on the stage of your microscope. Shine a bright light down on the mold. Be sure that the light does not also shine in your eyes and hinder your viewing. Use the low-power objective to examine the bread mold.

Note that the white cottony material is

What do molds look like? a tangled mass of filaments. This is called a *mycelium.* The threadlike growths are made of living matter. Trace one of the filaments. You will see that it runs horizontally for a short distance, then it branches into several vertical filaments. On the top of each of these vertical growths is a black knob. These are *sporangia,* or *spore cases.* Within each one of these cases are a large number of spores. Sooner or later, the knobs will burst open. The spores are so light that they will easily float away in the air. When a spore alights on some material that the mold can use for food, the spore will grow into a whole new mold plant. It was spores wiped up from the floor that grew into mold on your bread.

Directly beneath the vertical filaments are others that branch downward into the bread. These filaments act like roots by obtaining from the bread the nourishment the mold plant needs in order to live and grow.

Most molds are harmless to man, though

How are molds useful to man? a few may cause diseases. One such disease is "athlete's foot." Some molds are useful, such as the ones which give flavor to certain kinds of cheese. By far the most important use of molds is to provide the basis for the drugs called *antibiotics.* These drugs have helped to conquer certain diseases that took thousands of lives before antibiotics were discovered. Some antibiotics are penicillin, streptomycin, and aureomycin.

Having examined the mold on the bread by means of the low-power objective, examine it in a different way. Scrape some mold off the bread and place it on a glass slide. Add a drop of water and a drop of alcohol. Then cover it with a cover glass. Light the slide in the usual way; that is, by means of light reflected upward from the microscope mirror. First examine the mold with the low-power objective. Then use the high-power objective. You will see that each mold plant is made of many cells. You might even be able to see a nucleus in one of these cells.

It is possible that along with, or instead of, common bread mold, you will find an orange, black, green, or pink mold growing on your bread. Each color represents a different species of mold. Examine each one and make a comparison of the shapes and colors of the different parts of each mold.

Have you ever seen a whitish, powdery

What is mildew? material on shoes or leather jackets that were stored in a damp place? Or, perhaps, during a damp summer, you have seen the same kind of whitish spots on curtains or fabric furniture coverings. Or, you may have seen black streaks on sheets or pillow cases that your mother stored while they were still damp. Both the white spots and the black streaks were caused by *mildew,* which is the general name for a group of plants very much like true molds. Mildews have a mycelium and sporangia. Mildews not only stain and rot leather and cloth, but they also destroy many useful plants, among them roses,

SPORE CASE OF BREAD MOLD

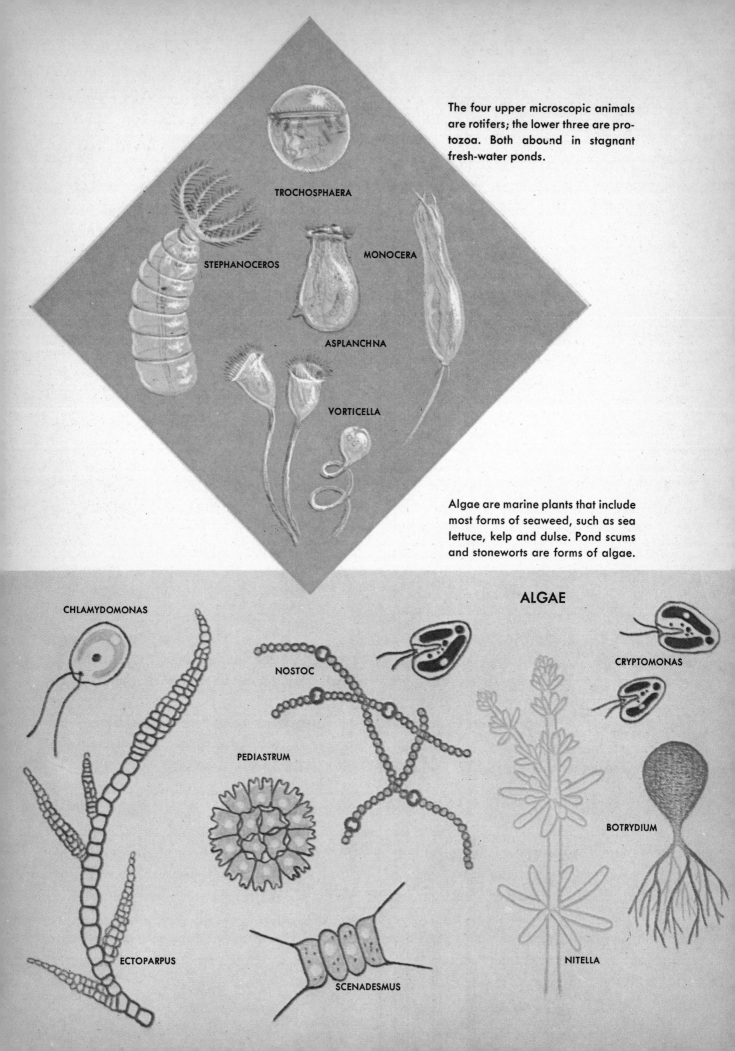

The four upper microscopic animals are rotifers; the lower three are protozoa. Both abound in stagnant fresh-water ponds.

TROCHOSPHAERA

STEPHANOCEROS

MONOCERA

ASPLANCHNA

VORTICELLA

Algae are marine plants that include most forms of seaweed, such as sea lettuce, kelp and dulse. Pond scums and stoneworts are forms of algae.

ALGAE

CHLAMYDOMONAS

NOSTOC

CRYPTOMONAS

PEDIASTRUM

ECTOPARPUS

SCENADESMUS

NITELLA

BOTRYDIUM

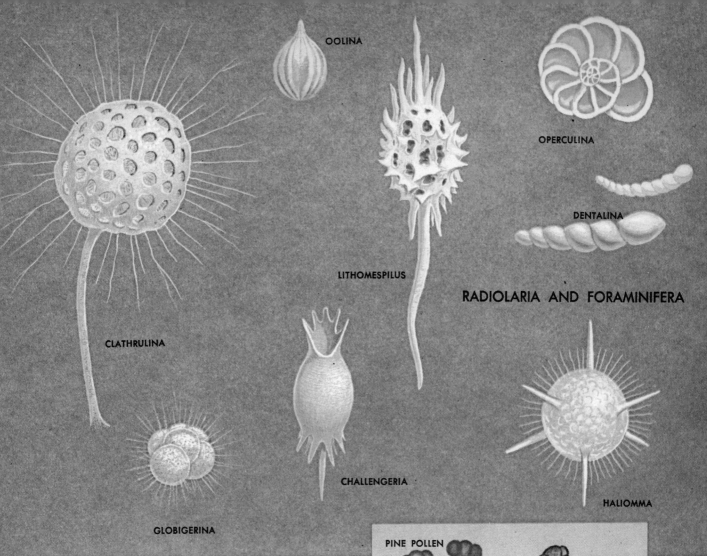

OOLINA

OPERCULINA

DENTALINA

LITHOMESPILUS

RADIOLARIA AND FORAMINIFERA

CLATHRULINA

CHALLENGERIA

HALIOMMA

GLOBIGERINA

Both *Radiolaria* and *Foraminifera* are shelled proto-zoa that live in the sea. Radiolaria have delicate glass-like shells. Foraminifera have chalk-like shells.

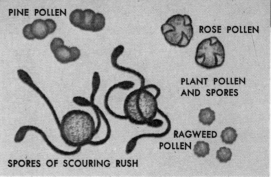

PINE POLLEN

ROSE POLLEN

PLANT POLLEN AND SPORES

RAGWEED POLLEN

SPORES OF SCOURING RUSH

Pollen grains have different shapes in different kinds of plants. Spores resist changes in heat and cold.

lilacs and willow, plum, cherry and peach trees. The mildew covers these plants with a mycelium through which it draws nourishment from the plant's cells. This destroys these cells, and therefore, kills the plant.

Observe mildew plants in the same way that you observed molds.

When you were feeding protozoa, you

What is yeast budding? made a mixture of yeast and water. Although you were primarily interested in the protozoa, you

may have noticed that the yeast cells had many curious shapes. Let us again observe yeast. As before, mix a tiny speck of yeast in a drop of water. Place a cover glass on the mixture. Manipulate the mirror of your microscope so as to cut down the light, and focus carefully on the yeast.

37

Yeast is a plant. The round, or nearly-round, cells that you see are each a separate yeast plant. Two things that will probably catch your attention immediately are that some yeast cells seem to have lumps sticking out of them, and that yeast cells are seen in chains. These two facts are closely related.

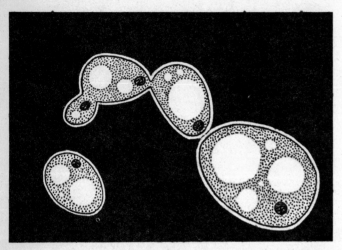

Yeast cells reproduce by a division called "budding."

Like other cells, yeast plants reproduce by cell division. But instead of dividing in two in the middle, a yeast cell grows a bud. This bud is the lump that you can see attached to some cells. Just as in other kinds of cell division, the nucleus splits in two. One part of the nucleus moves into the bud, and the other part remains in the parent cell. The bud is small at first, but soon grows to be the same size as the cell from which it budded. As you will remember, this is quite different from the type of cell division you have observed. There, the cell pinched in two, forming two cells each half the size of the cell that divided. Each of the two new cells then grew to the size of the cell from which they came.

How else does yeast budding differ from cell division? Another way in which the budding of yeast cells differs from most cell division is in the fact that the new cell which grows from the bud does not necessarily separate from the parent cell. Although the parent cell and the budded cell live as separate plants, they may remain attached to each other. As both these cells bud in turn, and the buds grow to full size, a chain of four cells is formed. Even longer chains of yeast cells may be formed. However, the connection between the cells is not very strong, and, eventually, the chain breaks.

If you search about among the yeast cells on your slide, you may find cells that have more than one bud. When this kind of budding takes place, Y-shaped chains may be formed.

How are yeasts useful to man? There are thousands of different kinds of yeasts. Certain kinds are very useful to man. These are the ones used in the process of *fermentation*. Most yeasts live and grow on sugar. As they obtain their nourishment from sugar, they change it into alcohol and carbon dioxide gas. This is the process called *fermentation*. Alcohol is a very useful chemical.

When yeast is mixed with baking dough, the yeast plants grow on the sugar in the dough. That is, the yeast ferments the sugar in the dough to form alcohol and carbon dioxide. This gas forms bubbles in the dough, and the dough swells. When this happens we say that the dough "rises." Dough that rises becomes light and fluffy. When the bread is baked, the heat drives off both the carbon dioxide and the alcohol. All the holes and indentations in a slice of bread are the remains of bubbles of carbon dioxide.

Dissolve a teaspoonful of sugar in half a tumbler of water. Make up a fresh mixture of yeast and water. Place a drop of the mixture on a cover glass and add a drop of sugar-water. Make a hanging-drop preparation of the cover glass and its mixture. Leave the hanging-drop slide in a warm place. An hour later, place the slide under your microscope. Do you see the many bubbles of carbon dioxide formed by the yeast's fermenting action on the sugar?

How can you see fermentation?

Insects

Obtain a small wide-mouth bottle with a lid. Cover the inside bottom with blotting paper, paper towels or absorbent cotton. Then wet the material with household ammonia. (Do not hold your face close to the bottle when you are pouring ammonia, for it will cause your eyes and nose to smart painfully.) Cap the wide-mouth bottle. Now you have an insect collector's bottle. If you place an insect in it, the ammonia will quickly kill the specimen without damaging it as swatting might do.

Where can you keep insects?

Catch a fly in your hand. When you see a fly resting on some object, slowly move your cupped hand close to the insect. Then, with a sudden quick movement, grab the fly. You will probably have to try this more than once. Hold the fly gently in your hand, and then pop it into the collecting bottle. After the fly is dead, use your tweezers to remove it from the bottle. Place it on a glass slide and manipulate it with your probe so that you can obtain a good view of one of its eyes beneath the low-power objective of your microscope.

Do you see that the whole surface of the eye is composed of tiny hexagonal (six-sided) spaces? These spaces are called *facets*. Each one gives the fly a separate impression of light and color. In other words, each facet acts as though it were a separate eye. An eye made up of facets is called a compound eye. Many insects have such eyes.

What does a fly's eye look like?

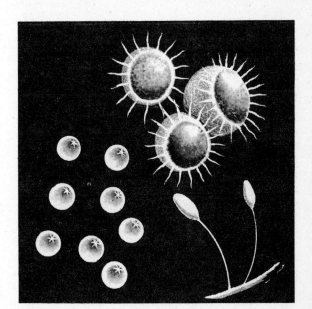

Insect eggs come in many different shapes and sizes.

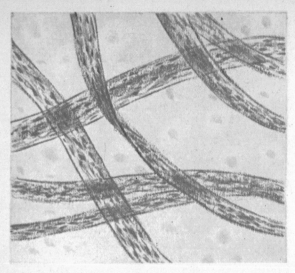
Orlon acrylic fiber, as seen under a microscope.

A filament of rayon yarn as seen under a microscope.

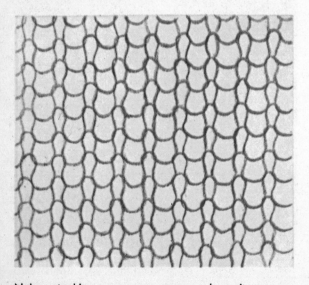
Nylon stocking weave as seen under microscope.

Note how the fly's eye bulges outward on all sides of the head. In fact the eyes make up the largest part of the head. Because the eyes bulge out so far, they enable the fly to see in all directions at once. This is why it is so hard to catch a fly, for it can see as well behind as in front of itself.

Look at the fly's foot. Note the hairy pads between two curving claws. The pads secrete a sticky substance that enable the fly to cling to smooth surfaces. This is why a fly can walk upside down on the ceiling. Look at the wings of a fly. The "veins" in the wing are really dried-up air tubes that connect with the fly's breathing organs.

How can a fly walk upside down?

There are more kinds of insects than any other kind of animal. As insects have an almost infinite variety of forms and oddly-shaped organs, a collection of several different kinds will provide you with enough material for many hours of interesting microscopic examination.

Fabrics

You may already know that cotton thread is made from the cotton plant. The fruit of the cotton plant is a white fluffy material much like absorbent cotton. This is cleaned and spun into thread. But just what goes on in the spinning process? You can find this out by examining a piece

How is cotton thread made?

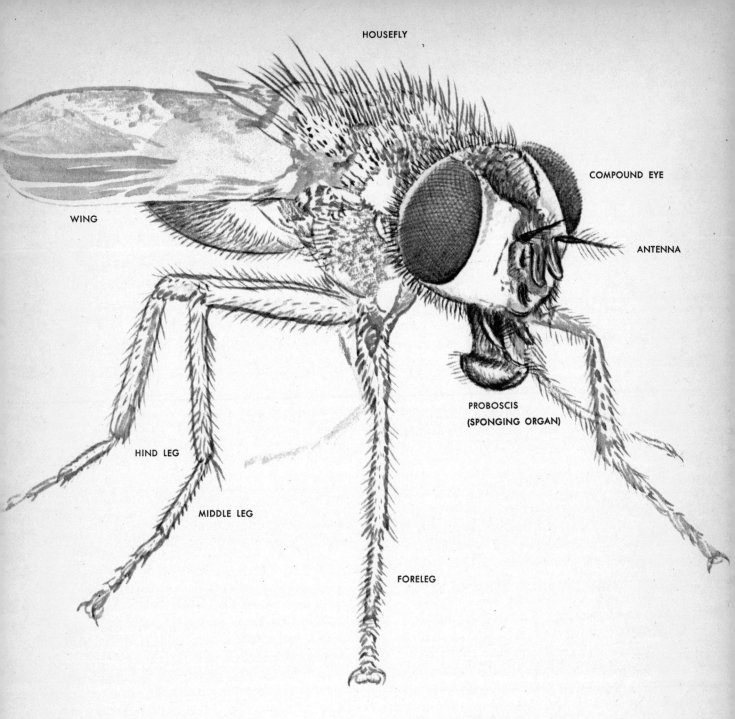

WING

COMPOUND EYE

ANTENNA

PROBOSCIS
(SPONGING ORGAN)

HIND LEG

MIDDLE LEG

FORELEG

of cotton thread under your microscope.

Make another probe by sticking the eye-end of a needle into the eraser from a pencil. Cut a half-inch length of cotton thread, wet it, and place it on a slide beneath the low-power objective of your microscope. Note that the whole length of the thread has a spiral twist.

Using both your probes, pick the thread apart. First undo the spiral, then pick the strands apart into the smaller fibers of which they are made. When you have taken the whole piece of thread apart, you can easily reconstruct what went on in the spinning process. The fibers that make up the cotton as it comes from the plant were pulled out into strands which were then twisted into a thread.

Since it is so easy to pick apart a piece of cotton, you may wonder what gives a thread its strength. Use a high-power objective to look at the smallest fibers. Do you see how crooked and twisted they are? When a number of these fibers are brought in close contact with one another, as in the cotton-spinning process, the crooked parts and bends of one fiber catch in the crooked parts of another and hold the separate fiber together.

Obtain a short length of wool yarn, silk thread and linen

How do natural fibers differ from man-made (artificial) ones?

thread. Examine each under the low- and high-power objectives of your microscope. Use direct lighting from above. Note that the wool fibers are straight, thick and scaly. Compare these wool fibers with a hair from your head. Note that the silk fibers are straight, but have rough surfaces. Linen fibers have very jagged surfaces. Do you think that there is any connection between the jagged surface of linen fibers and the strength of linen thread?

All the fibers you have examined so far are natural fibers. From the edges of the inside of a rayon, nylon, Orlon or Dacron garment, obtain a few threads. These are artificial or man-made fibers. Examine them under your microscope. Note how smooth they are when compared to natural fibers.

You can keep an interesting record of what you have learned by placing half-inch lengths of the four kinds of natural fibers on a glass slide, carefully covering them with a thin coating of Canada balsam and placing a cover

glass on the balsam. Do the same with the four kinds of man-made fibers.

Look at a muslin sheet or pillowcase

How is muslin woven?

with the low-power objective. Note how evenly the threads are woven into a square pattern. The weaving is done by stretching a large number of threads parallel to each other. These threads make the *warp*. An equal number of parallel threads are woven over and under, over and under the threads of the warp. The second group of threads is called the *woof*, or *weft*. Sometimes the over-and-under pattern of weaving is modified by having the woof go over two, three or more threads of the warp, before going under one thread. Try to obtain examples of rep and gabardine twill fabrics to examine under your microscope. Note how different from muslin the weave of these fabrics is.

Examine a jersey, T-shirt, or woman's

How is knitted fabric made?

stocking. The fabric from which these items are made is not woven, but is knitted. Examine a piece of felt from a man's hat or some other source. Can you see a weaving pattern here? There is none, for felt is not a woven cloth. It is made from a large number of short fur fibers that are mixed with water. The water is drained off, and the resulting mat is pressed flat.

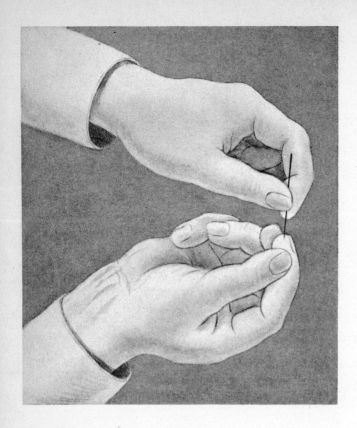

You can obtain a blood sample from the index finger of your hand with a sterilized needle.

Below are three steps in making a blood smear on a slide as indicated on page 44.

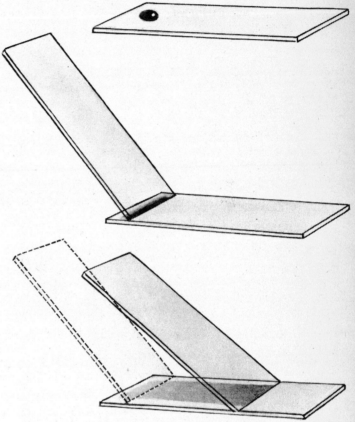

Blood

One of the most interesting things you **What does blood do?** can examine under a microscope is your own blood. Blood is a most remarkable fluid. It has been called "the river of life," and this is an excellent description, for blood supplies the cells of the body with the materials they need for nourishment and repair, and it removes wastes from the cells. Also, the blood contains cells that fight disease and substances that repair cut or bruised parts of the body.

Blood is made up of both liquid and **What is blood made of?** solid parts. The liquid is called *plasma*. The solid parts are *red corpuscles, white corpuscles,* and *platelets.* The word *corpuscle* is the Latin word for "little body." Corpuscles are cells. More than nine-tenths of the blood consists of red corpuscles. These cells are so small that a large drop of blood contains more than 250 million of them. They are disc-shaped and concave on each side, and contain a substance called *hemoglobin*. When hemoglobin combines with oxygen, it turns bright red. This is why fresh blood outside the body is always red.

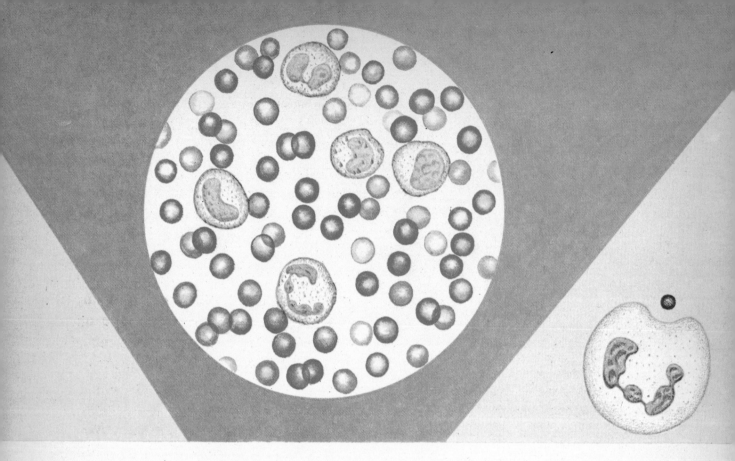

Let us examine some red cells. Set out

How can you get a sample of your blood?

two clean glass slides, some absorbent cotton, a bottle of hydrogen peroxide (usually called simply "peroxide"), a candle, a pair of tweezers, and a sharp needle. Light the candle. Scrub the tip of the index finger of your left hand (if you are right-handed) with a swab of peroxide-soaked cotton. Be thorough about this, in order to kill all bacteria on your fingertip. Hold this finger firmly between the thumb and middle finger of the same hand. Grasp the needle with the tweezers. Now, sterilize the point of the needle by holding it in the candle flame for 20 seconds. When the needle has cooled, grasp it near, but not at, the point. Quickly jab the needle into the index finger of your left hand — the one you have cleaned. This will hurt no more than a mosquito bite. Squeeze your finger in order to form a large drop of blood above the puncture. Before you go about taking a drop of your own blood, however, be sure to get permission from your parent or guardian. Also, you must be sure to have an adult supervise your whole experiment.

With your right hand, pick up one of

How do you make a blood smear?

the clean slides and touch it, near one end, to the drop of blood. Place this slide on a table, with the drop of blood uppermost. Hold this slide firmly between the thumb and middle finger of your left hand. Pick up the other slide in your right hand. Hold it nearly vertical and touch its bottom edge to the drop of blood on the first slide. Rapidly and smoothly move the nearly-vertical slide along the surface of the other slide,

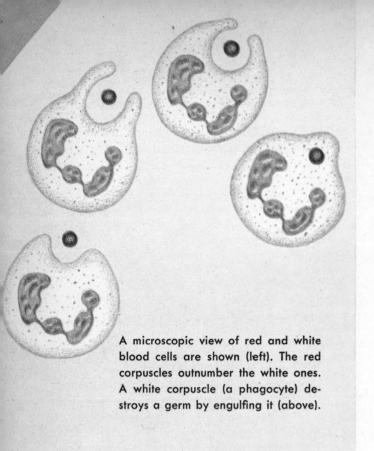

A microscopic view of red and white blood cells are shown (left). The red corpuscles outnumber the white ones. A white corpuscle (a phagocyte) destroys a germ by engulfing it (above).

cells standing on edge and resembling dumbbells. There may be several red cells stacked one on top of another like a pile of coins.

Here and there among the red cells, you will see a much larger, colorless cell. These are white corpuscles. There is only one white corpuscle for approximately every 800 red corpuscles. Most of these cells have a generally round shape, but they may be in almost any shape, looking very much like an amoeba. In fact, they are able to move through the body's tissues in much the same manner as an amoeba moves. White cells are the body's disease fighters, and disease is caused by an over-abundance of harmful bacteria within

pulling the blood in an even smear along behind the moving slide. Study the illustration to understand clearly how to do this. You must do all this quickly, so that the drop of blood on the slide does not clot before you spread it out into a smear.

When you have finished making the blood smear, swab off your left index finger with peroxide-soaked cotton.

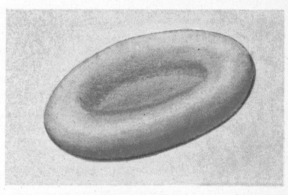

One red blood cell, or corpuscle, shown magnified.

Examine the blood smear under the low-power objective.

What do blood cells look like? The red cells will look barely pink. Move the slide back and forth in order to get an idea of how many thousands of red cells are in the small drop of blood you put on the slide.

Now, use the high-power objective. You can easily see that red cells are circular with a concave depression in the middle of each side. You may see some

the body. It is the task of white corpuscles to destroy bacteria. To destroy a bacterium, a white cell engulfs it, just as an amoeba engulfs a bit of food. Inside the white cell, the bacterium is digested.

A special kind of stain is needed to properly stain a white cell, but you can do a fairly good job by using "permanent" blue fountain pen ink. When you have fixed and stained your blood smear, you will see that white corpuscles have very irregularly-shaped nuclei. The nucleus may be round, somewhat horse-shoe-shaped, or made up of several small bits held together by threads of nuclear material. It is because of the shape of the nucleus, that a white cell is called a *polymorphonuclear leucocyte*. *Poly* means "many" in Greek; *morphos* means "form"; *leuco* means "white"; and *cytos* means "cell." Thus, the big word means "white cell with many-formed nucleus."

Get a piece of thin wood about three inches long and two **How can you see blood in circulation?** inches wide. A piece of plywood will do, or a shingle. Near one end, drill a hole about a half-inch in diameter. Make a pad of wet cloth or

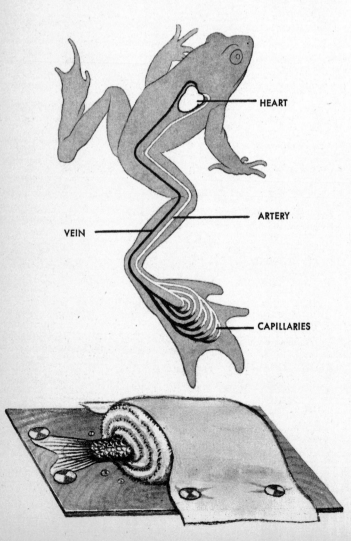

HEART

ARTERY

VEIN

CAPILLARIES

absorbent cotton about five by ten inches. Gently wrap a live goldfish in this pad, so that only its tail sticks out. Put the fish on the board in such a position that the tail-fin is directly over the hole. Place a handkerchief over the upper part of the fish and fix the handkerchief to the board with thumbtacks. Place two other thumbtacks at the edges of the hole so that the edges of the tacks press on the two outer points of the fish's tail. Be careful not to stick the tacks through the tail.

Place the board on the stage of your microscope, with the tail directly under the objective. Focus with low power. As you examine the tail, wet it from time to time with a little water from your fingers.

You will see large blood vessels that run parallel to the rays of the tail. Note how these large vessels divide into smaller branches, and these branches into tiny ones, called *capillaries*. If you follow the flow of blood cells from the large blood vessels to the capillaries, you will see that from the capillaries, the blood flows into larger branches that join still larger blood vessels, as the blood flows back to the fish's heart.

Do not keep the fish out of water for more than ten minutes. If, when you return the fish to water, it seems sluggish and unable to swim well, pick it up by the tail and dip it in and out of the water a few times. This should help the fish to begin breathing properly again.

The flow of blood may be viewed in a frog's foot as it travels from the heart, through the arteries and capillaries and back to the heart through the veins. The blood flow may also be viewed in a fish's tail.

Suppose you are interested in learning

How can you observe the insides of living things?
about the heart of a frog, the stem of a flower, or the egg of an insect. After you have examined these objects with the low- and high-power objectives of your microscope, you can still learn much more about them by studying their insides. What is the best way to do this?

Obtain a bolt that is at least one-quarter inch in diameter, and a nut to fit the bolt. Screw the bolt about one-quarter way into the nut. Prop the bolt in a vertical position, so that the opening in the bolt is uppermost. Place the object you wish to study inside this opening. Melt some paraffin — the material used to seal jam and jelly jars — in a spoon, using a candle flame for a source of heat. Pour the melted paraffin into the hole in the bolt.

When the paraffin has cooled and hardened, slowly screw the bolt farther into the nut, thereby pushing out some paraffin. When about 1/64 of an inch (or less) of paraffin has been pushed out, move a razor blade down along the face of the bolt, so as to cut off a thin

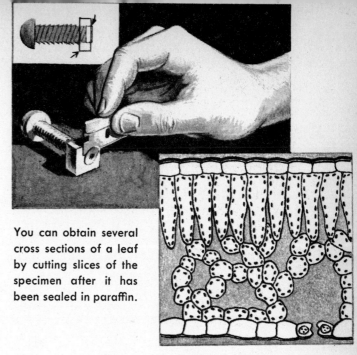

You can obtain several cross sections of a leaf by cutting slices of the specimen after it has been sealed in paraffin.

slice of paraffin. If this slice contains a portion of your specimen, place the slice on a slide and examine it under the microscope. If not, then push out another 1/64 of an inch of paraffin. Continue this until one of the slices contains a piece of the specimen. Then, go on making more slices until you have passed from one end to the other of the specimen. Each slice shows you a cross section, revealing what is inside the object under study.

If your specimen is too large to be put into the hole in a bolt, use some other small container, such as a match box.

The Electron Microscope

Both the simple and compound micro-

What are the limitations of optical microscopes?
scopes are called *optical* microscopes. They both use light to present an enlarged image to the eye. But no matter how powerful optical micro-

scopes are made, there is a limit to the smallness of the object that they can magnify. We learned that light must be reflected from an object in order for it to be seen. Objects also can be seen when they stop the passage of light, as when they make a shadow; and also when they partially stop the passages of light, as when light passes up from a microscope's mirror through the body of a protozoan. Light rays have a certain definite size, and they cannot be reflected from or stopped by objects that are smaller than the rays themselves. To try to see objects that are smaller than the light rays is like trying to catch minnows with a mackerel net.

A scientist operates a powerful electron microscope.

If we could have some kind of ray, or beam, that could be reflected from objects too small to reflect light, we could see these objects. There are tiny particles, called *electrons*, that are sufficiently small for our purpose. Scientists have worked out a way to use a beam of electrons in a microscope. This microscope is called an *electron microscope*.

What is an electron microscope?

By heating a certain kind of wire, a large number of electrons may be obtained. Electrons are electrically charged particles. By using magnets in exactly the same way an optical microscope uses lenses, the electrons obtained from the wire can be formed into a beam, to be directed and magnified.

Since eyesight requires light, we cannot look into an electron microscope as we do an optical one. But the beam of electrons can form an image on photographic film. When the film is developed, we see what was beneath the electron microscope's objective.

With this instrument, we can get magnifications of more than 200 thousand times, but because an electron microscope costs several thousand dollars,

it is usually found only in university and industrial research laboratories.

One of the great triumphs of the electron microscope has been to reveal viruses, the smallest living things. Viruses cause many diseases, among which are measles, mumps, chickenpox, smallpox, rabies and polio. The electron microscope may help us to conquer disease by enabling us to work with viruses.

How does this microscope help man?

You have learned something about the world of very small things that exist all around us. You have learned about a wonderful instrument, the microscope, that has enabled man to enter this tiny world. You have learned how to use a microscope and how to obtain and prepare very small specimens so that you can observe them with this important instrument.

But if what you have learned has aroused an interest in the "unseen world," then ahead of you are endless, invaluable hours of fun and learning.